# In an Attic Palace Beneath a Slaughtered Sky

# In an Attic Palace Beneath a Slaughtered Sky

## John Greiner

ARTEIDOLIA
PRESSPRESSPRESSPRESSPRESS

New York

In an Attic Palace Beneath a Slaughtered Sky

Special thanks to Word For/Word,
The Rye Whiskey Review,
Good Cop/Bad Cop Press, Literary Underground,
Gambling the Aisle, The Blue House,
Punk Noir Magazine and
Pax Americana, where a selection of the
works in this book originally appeared.

Décollage · John Greiner
Book design · Arteidolia Press

ARTEIDOLIA PRESS
P.O. Box 157
New York, N.Y. 10276

arteidolia.com/arteidolia-press

First Edition
Library of Congress Control Number: 2021922348
ISBN: 978-1-7369983-2-8

# contents
# CONTENTS
# contents
# contents
# CONTENTS
# contents

# Fairytale

Having forgotten
all of the fairytales
that had been told
to me in my youth
I decided to find
an antiquarian
who was well
versed in the dusty
tomes that make up my life.

The finding of such
a person was achieved
far more easily
than I had hoped.
It was my desire
to learn more
than a few things
along the way.
The pursuit being
the perfect
teacher of things passed.
I had packed my bags
for the long journey.
Sadly, I am no hero
of Greek proportions,
and this in spite
of the fire
that I had swallowed
on the boardwalk
at Coney Island
as Homer looked on laughing.

When I stepped out off
of my eighth story
balcony I fell upon
a stake that had
just been set-up that

very day.  Being
that no substantial
damage was caused
by my impalement,
the owner was delighted
at my arrival.
In fact such an arrival
was what he had often
longed for, and in
setting up shop in such
an unfamiliar neighborhood
he was vindicated
in the one great dream
that had consumed
him for so many years.

From the look of surprise
on my face after such
a clean collapse, devoid
of anything more
than a minor loss of blood,
he could immediately
discern what I had
dropped in for.

There it was, dusty
and frayed,
just the way that I
had imagined it.
Opening the book
I laughed at the cautionary
tales that I had once
held sacred, but with
age had come
to disregard.

All the dead and dying
faces of the children
who had far less
luck than I with

scissors and matches
lay waiting for the grave.
The tall shopkeeper
could not help
but shout with delight
and amazement while
slicing a thick
piece of salami
on the counter.
He asked if I would like
to join him for lunch.
How could I refuse?

We laughed at all
of the saccharine stories
that are fed to youths
these days on dry
pieces of toast, and of
how when push
comes to shove
these same children
are snipped
from life's long lie
by sharp scissors.
We gave great grins
at the babes
who go up in flames
laughing at the orange
glow and blistering
skin not realizing
that the end is the only
cause for the beginning.

My stomach full,
I climbed the fire escape
back up to the eighth story
promising the antiquarian
to return the next day,
but the following morning
when I slammed down

onto the street
he was no longer there
though the spike remained.
We had both
achieved what
we had wanted,
and that being
the case there was no
reason to stick around
and watch for what
would happen next.

## Razor for Rimbaud

I prefer scum, gunrunner,
       slave trader, pimp,
       customer service rep,
       switchblade slicer
through Times Square castrating
       tourists and lights,
       crooked cabbie
       lacking change,
9th Avenue whore, Coney Island
       clown, busker
       on the 3 a.m. train,
scheister, charlatan, tarot card
       reader in shop
       front window,
bloody butcher, moaning cow,
       Meat Packing District
       hostess to the stars,
       blowjob queen and evangelist
over all precious and impotent
poets of pristine days.

I take shits on presidents,
          premiers
and potentates in Park Avenue
hedge fund counting houses.
I set fire to the classics
       and classrooms,
they're all the same to me,
which is nothing.
I fly into the crowd
to spin around
       with knuckles
ready to bleed.

This is the razor song to sheer
the wallowing words from the page.

## View

Sought in the song lost in the port
    landing here
where rooms are left empty
except for the birds' eyes
     above
ships and sailors don't stay long
they leave too soon and are lost to the sea
not to be thought of
beyond the farewell wave
       the ceiling fan shudders
as the air comes up with excuses
       to exit
         through the window
all the animals that we have known on this island
do not live up to their skin
their stories are less interesting than that
        of the tanner's
still we go out
every evening
looking for a corner
to turn down
and find the land of rest
if not
    back to the room
    with the birds' eyes viewing
    to look up on
down by the piers where the better dancers
wait to dive in to cool after a long night
there is talk of someone winning the lottery
and not having to put forth sweat anymore
      on the floor
such a religion is for the sufferers
    whose knees
have held the weight of standing faith
    for too long
this island lacks consequence
it is being overrun by billionaires
who are nothing more than the victims

                    of plunging skies
passing for heaven
they are the failings of the land
the subjects of brief laughs
in their eternity
that falls far short of the price paid

                              I with the murderers
                              see the antique stars
                              in the skies
                              that have already died

bright wishes are being pimped
in spite of it all
to the mothers in their labor pains

## At the Other End of the Line

At the other end
of the line
where the train
finds fulfillment
in the death
of it travels
the passengers
are waiting
for an airplane,
unsatisfied.
No doubt
they will demand
a flight to the moon
by the time
the day is done.
That's of no concern
to the conductor
who has his knife
at the ready.
Once the railroad
fulfilled further
ambitions
that ended
in seasickness
and a fear
of submarines.
Now it's nothing,
but nothing
is greater than
the disappointment
of looking up
at clouds
hurrying by.

## Sheepshead Bay

The hallowed scum of the sea quivers.  Your children fear too many things while sleeping with stingrays on winter nights.  They shock you and everyone else who run to the city for solstice.  Your children are the fishers of fish and should never indulge in greater ambitions.  Your womb is a seashell where you hide sound and bury my scissors.  The boardwalk lusts for Sheepshead Bay.

# Tilt-a-Whirl

The drop
of a brick, tilt-a-whirl thrill.
The songstress has no voice,
never had, and that's
    the short and long of it
        in chit-chat
under the boardwalk,
out of the sun
where they're promising fun.
Still, one show is pretty
      much the same as the next,
especially for me, never one
       for discernment.
All of the degrees of summer
    didn't matter in September
    and mattered all the less
by the time that the spring came
    and February said goodbye.
No vocal coach.
No concern for all the suitors
   to be.
No worry about harmony or dissonance.
Let's sway into the jackhammer age
and lend a hand to the hydraulic masturbator
while Salvation Army ladies work their wrists
   knowing that Christmas
   is always right around the corner.
There are no venial sins here.
Each and every act is mortal.
Bright glare the days fade beneath amusement's
            lights.

## Lecture I

Heralding
　　holistic zeitgeist
　　　　you'll see
　　　　　　it points
to the steps.　The impressions
　　more important
　　　　　　than ideas.
To become a whole
　　discern who's
　　　　playing
the interesting
　　　exercises.
Monologues
　　meshing.
　　　　How it's
　　　　　said is
　　　　　　meticulous.
The last paragraph
　　melts down
　　　　the epitome
　　　　　of the indelible.
Who says so?
The Sunday *Times*.
What qualifies?
　　　It's a topic of debate.
So
　distracting.
　　　Look!
Apollonian and Dionysian.
　　　Ok.
　I've covered it all.
New icons
　　are a long time
　　　study
that arrives
　　at minimalism
　　　in a
tree stump.

## The Bible of my Nursery Rhymes

The sweep of your
fin de siècle dress
into the next century
and the century after that
left the historians in tatters
I was looking
      for the best tea party in town
        the Queen of Hearts
          Dr. Hoffmann
            my red shoes
and my bible of nursery rhymes
but settled on your solicitation
and promises of a future
where two nickels equal
      more than a dime
after an hour I was a dollar short
of all the ambitions of the epoch
and the empire that it dreamed
not to mention that there was no
currency exchange about willing
to give me a good rate for my pound
              of flesh
I offered to buy you a lemonade
and sit by your side on the terrace
      while the sun set
but watching the sun set
had never been one of your pursuits
it bored you
you said

## Avignon

Step aside with a shrug
of the shoulder
there's no need
for the big game to be played.
From the airport
comes another hero
too good for the ground,
still he's stuck here.
I knew a linebacker once
who was always in the way.
He got a Super Bowl ring
and once that happened
no one stepped aside.
It was no good for his sense of self.
He thought he was a phantom.
All these birds falling from the sky
would prefer to be looked upon as legends.
They melt at the sight of the sun,
envious of its every flame.
These are things that troubadours
sing about once they fall
off of the truck to Avignon.

# Breakup This Bit of Meaning

Break
     Up
This bit
     Of mean
Ing
     Ness
     Less
Lousy
     Clap
     Trap
Mouth
Caught
     Dry
     Cheese
While
We
Starve
No
     Re-
In
     Creation
Just
Fall
     Ing
Waters
     Back
Dead
Architect
To cure
The cause
     For
Child
     Hood
Dreams
     Of
          Ma
          Pa
On Christmas

Mourn
Ing
For
The day
Of the
Dead's

Lost
Soul
And
Presence
In
Threadbare
Stockings
Of
Depression
Era
Stirring
In the
Dust
Bowl
Of never
Promised
Land
Anger
Arises
In the
Cry
Mea
Of dead
Shores
Charge
A light
Brigade
With wild
Whistling
Wind
Death
Chants
Charted
On

Dry

Ground

Far from

The sea

Where

It was

Said

So much

To been

Seen

Such promises

Clash

With the real

It

Y

Of yes

And no

Concern

For these

Thoughts

That

Set

History

Down

In

The grey

Matter

Minus

Tenny's

Son

And oranges

Or tangerines

On

The

Holiday's

Morn

As the

Ash

Es

Scatter over

The

Short
    En
        Ed
Which gives
        No
            Bread
Of survival
        To
        The
Reader
    Whose
        Vocab
            You
        Larry
And
    Stooges
Is
    Best
        Left
            Served
In the
    Hiero
        Glyphics
Of trance
        Shamed
            Men
Of bygone
    Epochs.

## My Russian Bride

Lead me out by your gold chain. I'm not afraid of your Big Bad Wolf. I've clawed many a nighttime song and set them on my lap silent. We'll go into the woods and scare up the witches of winters past. Remember to bring your knife. Remember to stay out of the sight of the moon. You leave me longing for the mornings that I loathe. You resemble my Russian bride, frozen before the revolution ever began.

# Miss Americana

## I

Unfurl       me       flung       out
    for

        flag

## A – MER – I – CA

    I'm yours
virgin  perpetuity  princess

    I'm the comprehension
        of your cross
bare  bone  sucker  punch      lady
                        lusty
                        liberty
I'm your captain
      come down    project(ed)
                   reborn
                   revelation
                   rebirth
between the mediocrity
   and the madness            falls the nation
                  sail           Atlantic
     and       I       my
                  saw          Pacific
             ship(ped)
                   Manifest
destiny in the depth
     dark
      plunge
                 read       comic book
     and       I       my
                  bleed      project(ed)

      on the big screen

in the time of the small
            and mean
while the text is incinerated

I pledge allegiance.

## II

I'm your nightmare auditor
your financial man
the backdoor lounger
        low on the totem poll
        up on the stage
        shivering in the spotlight
busted           your Don Juan
                    JU
                    an
        like Byron clubfooted
                        but with calculator

        at the ready
Casanova cum Steve Rogers
        of the skin flick
                    blink               born on the Fourth of July
        in the booth                   on the Lower East Side
                    now
        tomorrow
                    no tokens
the ecstasy of history
consumed in the victory
the wailing women writhe
                    on the cutting room floor
no more two-bits for peace

        an eviscerated
                        soft shell
            before the sensuous blank screen

bled                        out
                            blood        red white
                blue
                seed-y

20

sorrow
and futures of fantasy       that could never     be
     placed.

## III

I sleep in                spurts
    between shootings
      in
      the cinema
          longing
           for
          the screen
and jerkoff       praise         spraying
     transcendental       pipeline ending

in Arctic salvation

Smoking bath in the bay it's a complete mess
so I'll filter bad breath in the garlic field
of your promise shined by the sea

      Those are all of the third eyes blind
my Miss
     Americana
I knew your speech
before the angels
even started to sing
I knew their song
from the past fifteen
Super Bowls' halftime
     sorrows

Kiss me
my Miss
     Americana

# AT LEAST ON THE FOREHEAD

like a good mama
        remembering the vitality
of the womb

before        it        was                the        big
        break                                minute        after
            in                    the
                                moment
                        of
            disappointment
                            at      last.

This is the at last
The shoot out at the theater
The Friday morning dying
        that will be forgotten
        by Friday next

Burned in to fizzle out

Through the head
No need for shock
Never a need for shock

# Acclimatized
# A – MER – I – CA

The numbing screens
                        ubiquitous
update personal frailties
                        until the finish
No need.

## IV

Phony Bam!
Playing to the hope.

Fake    fake    fake    fake    goose

Don't crucify me
Don't lynch me
Don't castrate me
          between the pages
Don't fence me in.
I'd fall for Emma Goldman
          in Union Square shouting
not these muddled headed
                    handkerchief
                    hidden
anarchy babies of the modern day
who don't know the names
                    Bakunin
                    Kropotkin
                    Proudhon
Who never tossed a    Molotov
                              cocktail
bandana bumpkins
little freaks without the deak
faces masked in the shade
                    rattled          brain          ramblers
now fools of 14th Street


I'm gone in the epic opera
          pounding in the harbor
waiting to drown the earth
during the World Series   seventh inning.    take me out
                    stretched thin.     before the curtains fall
                    scream no more    on the final movement
through songs and psalms and symphonies
                    heroic


Wave goodbye.
          Stephen Foster in Bellevue ward with beautiful
                    dreamers broke
          Scott Joplin syphilitic rage and rag of Wall Street
                    dementia while waiting for a pauper's grave
          Robert Johnson swilling strychnine from an opened
                    whiskey bottle
          Bix Beiderbecke sweating the dagger wielding Mexicans

hiding beneath the bed
George Gershwin gone from Tin Pan Alley to Hollywood
hosanna blinding headache no more shall we dance
Hank Williams in the back of a Cadillac sleeping
through the never ending New Year's Day
and the one thousand rock-n-roll suicides
and the one thousand rock-n-roll suicides to come.

## V

Blow my head
Beam me up
Stop busting my balls
and give me a good ball
Miss Americana
and I'll fall on foreign fields            for you
and only for you


just give me an hour on your kingdom's big brass bed
without the fakes
and the phonies
and the bugles' taps
diminishing the return
I'm ready for my birthday cake
Next year beyond the horizon
and heavenly conceits

I'll dance with you
around the Washington Monument
and then take a seat on Abe Lincoln's lap
with a good view of all the glories

Merry makers wailing
walled out                              prayers
whisper
two-bit     peace     tokens
princes
presidents
and                press secretaries
primp in the closets                          darkly
fouled                              delighted

Prayers always forgotten once fulfilled
and then comes the flip backwards
and the next kid gets kicked in the head
                    for a hundred years that seem forever
                                        that are forever
because he's the eternal child of expiation
                    until expired


Give it to me, Miss Americana
                    you are the soaring sex fiend
I pledge my midnights bound and sweaty to


Give it to me, Miss Americana
                    you're the scream queen
who put history in her place, sniveling


You've got the loaded dice
          my              my              my
                Miss            Americana
          my              my              my

## A – MER – I – CA
                    I'm ready.

# Mary Magdalene

The sleep stream has slipped away
and they are stoning the good girl.
No one was ready for the sun
to be so unforgiving
in its come up.
The swaying dancers, stiffening,
are in the basement
along with all of their good intent.
The present remains
unconcerned with what's hidden.
Having lost their wings
the flies are here to amuse,
still no one is happy
I am glad for the doctor
that has come for the good girl,
though she will be of no use to anyone.
There was never a tooth
that I regretted the loss of.
There's no bite left in the end
that we have scripted for ourselves.

# Coal Chute

I broke through the window
with the moon bawling
the sound filled the avenue

the leaves on the one tree
left standing on the corner
broke loose and fell to the ground

my eyes had rusted over
and I started to scratch at the sky
cursing clouds that wished to pass

the shards of glass that lay on the floor
would be a gift for the pawnbroker
something to get him through the bright hours

the wind sent a chill through the bedroom
the dancers nursed their injured legs
in a room down the hallway without lamps

candles and flashlights were never my thing
my eyes shine with the glare of Jehovah
it's good to be one of the anointed

the ballroom was the center of my thoughts
my scalp covered an attic palace with an orchestra on payroll
dreams filled the bank books of the holy rollers

seeing her among so many
I recognized that I would never again sleep
on the beach waiting for the ocean to rise

cast down the coal chute of a long gone time
I knew that I would show up
sullied and cheerful somewhere else in this world

# This I Did

I
did.
I
lost
  trying
not to.
This I did,
but I did not
want to do.
It was done
like a tooth
being pulled,
a car crash,
a hat being
dropped from
the side of a boat
into the Black Sea,
or a justice
of the peace
          with a
Kaiser Wilhelm
moustache
shooting
at a bride and groom
after being paid
for his services
on their wedding day.
Like that
it was done
and in doing it
nothing was gained;
I still have all
of my yellowing teeth
in spite of
my dental hygienist's
          passions,
my car
is still in Henry Ford's

vital skull
in a marvel of Michigan
          cemetery,
my hat
will never drown
off of the Turkish shores
with wild dogs barking,
it rages against
          the rain,
and the justice of the peace
takes cash calmly, kindly,
thinking only of suicide
and all of the divorces
          to come,
but I,
I
did
though
I
did not
want to do
and
I
lost
  trying
which only validated
my faith
in the pleasure
of naught.

## Your Filth is a Palace

Your filth is a palace
Where kicked up dust
Brings fulfillment
To my tender desires.

Your rotting teeth
Are the stumps of dreams
That I have always
Longed to devour.

Your scars are a road map
To paradise that saints
Have never dared to examine
In their rush for salvation.

The cataracts on your eyes
Are the remnants
Of visions that Tiresias
Hoped to see fulfilled.

You are love reneged,
And you are the dead
Flowers that perfume
The universe.

I will sit out eternity
By your side
Singing softly
Into your deaf ears.

# Rue St. Denis

Dancing girl with empty glass
in her flurry
                broke the Hungarian's back.
I was there.
with a half finished requiem
            all my own
                    that I couldn't
            whistle in peace,
            so I decided to leave it for Sunday morning
                        mass.
Outside
the broken boy
                dragged himself across the street
on wooden legs.
It wasn't for me
to catch his show.
I cracked my own
            empty glass
            and was warned
            that the Romanian impresario
would rage, this being his café.
What a way to run a business,
that was all I had to say
and started to hum
while waiting for the waltz to
            kick-up.  They abhorred
            the Viennese, so I
            decided to exist
                    in histrionic tears.
            My recitative of *La Marseillaise*.
brought the
house down.
Caught up,
the dancing girl stopped
                in her tracks,
and handed her
glass over to the
                wandering waiter
                hoping he'd join
her in the swirl.

## Sunday F Train Running all the way to Stillwell Avenue

Conscious of your pig pen skull
I lunge deep into Sunday morning
my lighter the sun that brings the sky down
I spit straight in the face
of the funny man up above
while they look and talk
and give all of the goods that a God damn
can get you if you do more than just say
so and so and get down into the theosophy of it
they play it straighter than the farmer in the dell
that's some story that's told about him
and the muck where he ended up
fun loving agriculturalist that he was
your skull tidy as it's not
is a circus of freak show delights
I look at it this minute in the lust
life made up of a million
dizzying instances of good grace and bad
teeth that get worse with rotting
the local train is chasing me all the way
down to Coney Island and there's going
to be a big and bloody crash when it crosses
paths with the Cyclone but I will be fine
sitting out this Sunday with you and your
pig pen skull on the beach after the wells
at Ruby's wash our better manners away

## It is Raining and Violent in Paris

It is raining and violent in Paris
      this spring
the French Open is a fiasco
undermined by complaints
the Seine has flooded
this room reminds me of the bar
      at the Meurice
though it looks nothing like it
I have always preferred the Meurice
to the Ritz and the Crillon
but on this sunny spring day
      in New York City
my preference for the Meurice
over the Ritz and the Crillon
      is of no importance
for it is violent and raining
      in Paris
where the French Open is in ruins
and the Seine has overflowed its banks

## The Slaughter of the Skies

In the east there are daydreams
of cowboys looking out with teary
eyes on all of the conquests
they never had the courage to run
after with the blood lust of the braver lot
       hell bent on a holocaust.
They will tell you otherwise, of course,
as they slaughter the skies.

## To the Top of the World

The pennies on the eyes of the northern skies
can't buy you anything that you need,
so it's better to stay blind as you slip down
                 the side of the world.
We're for different shores.
These states and sounds
drain the blood from the lips.
I'm running short
on all of the time that I borrowed.

# The Card Player

I held a low hand
raised a pipe
skipped dinner
shunned kids
despised wife
grew my moustache long
left the field
cursing the farm
wished for a better day
folded
convulsed angrily
before regaining composure
asked for a match
blew smoke rings
counted my change
threw in my chips
imagined my face calm
raised
hoped
and cleared
the table

## The Hat

Antoine fled the scene
In such a rush
That he left
His top hat
Behind
On the call girl's
Phone book
Which sat next
To the bed
Bug's breakfast.
It was a great
Embarrassment to Antoine
Being that the hat
Was worth more
Than the girl,
And that it
Was not even
His hat, rather
It was his uncle's
Valet's
Who had that Saturday off,
And who would
Have to travel
To the cathedral
Bareheaded
On Sunday
Scorned
By servants,
And masters
Alike.

## Walk About

The walk about
in the street
with this threadbare
coat leaves me
with a memory
of my hat.
I hate windy days
and the ill planned
games they have led
me to.
I am a poor sport
and a bad runner.
I was never made
for this race.
I am the friend of mice
who can not find
their way to the paradise
the glee makers set up.
The shock of the same
has left me balding
and cursing umbrellas.
In spite of it all,
further corners
and their endless
cross streets
leave me cold.

# Blue Laws

Stayed in the streets
and away from the wonder
           of the far gone
caught on the tongue
with a blade of word
        razor straight
my beard isn't much today
           the barber
           being barred
           from giving
           shaves
           on Sundays
the blue laws save someone's soul
but not the lord's
lost on the street
picked up
by the would be
        who has spoken to save
and places mouth wide around the word
waiting for the razor
hangmen stand around
           laughing
as if tomorrow will never come
with a deaf ear
         longing
the windows are left open
the ladies shout down their farewells
widows they will be after wonderment
has been left behind the wall
and they wander off
caution will be called upon
by those who witness their roam
             out
               beyond the lands
               where the woods
               catch dark

crucifixions not witnessed
it is lonely up there

the ladder hidden in the heart having been lost
those left hold out for a cardiac arrest
lacking heroics in their exit
no need to wash your hands
before the rise up in the world
dirty thoughts astonish

## A View of Paris with Furtive Pedestrians

You
with your yellow
window shade
pulled tightly shut
are more beautiful
                than
the waitress
who lives
in the room
                        below
                    You
        with her drained
        blue sky
        window white
        this rainy day brilliant
lazily removing
                    brilliance
You
are not
as gorgeous
as the line cook
                above
                beneath
the mansard roof
and bursting
with someday
                maybe
Wednesday
                sun
I
could never leave
You
You
have made me weary
        of long climbs up
                    narrow
stairwells
                        once
                        however

                    I made
                    love
to the waitress
                    below
she
enveloped
me
in first floor
ascension dreams
I was born a blueblood
with dirty grey blinds
a dusty suite
a stained toilet bowl
a pinstriped suit
and an account
                    at
the ground floor restaurant
        I am
happy with their advertised
        *plats chauds*
although
I have never felt
                    a
        plate
        hot to the touch
on the premises
I always eat
                    lavender
                    sorbet
for dinner
which causes me
to shiver
                            uncontrollably
                    in
the October
        through
    March
street
longing for You
to pull up your blind
open Your window
                            and wave

42

## Traveling Salesman on the Somewhere Road to Home

Judging by the laughter
that filled the room
I was able to tell
that there were more
aching hearts
than I had the mind
to sell work boots
and ball gowns to.
It's rough on the road
trying to move merchandise
that's not even a step up
from a sweatshop seamstress's
hand me downs.
I was told that a salesman,
once he gets going,
gets all of the loving darlings.
I'm not going to say
that 's incorrect.
It's more a matter of it
not being what it's cracked
        up to be.
I should have been
a train conductor,
or a comedian
at the burlesque house
at the edge of New Jerusalem.
All of the laughter
and aching hearts
that flooded that room
made it hard
to get a foot in the door,
let alone my tongue
out of the mouth.

## Apartment

One pair
two, but
a truly full
    teaspoon
      fits
   a volume.
Alternative;
   spinning on drywall screws.
Association an
    empty
      landscape
    for
      another exploration.
A little later you
   recognize the sound.
Strange rumblings,
sighing,
gasping.
   Vapors flow along the floor,
   penetrate and quickly lift.
        Disposable.
        Extraordinary.
Help me out.
   Spots.
   Objects.
   Sounds.
We heard.
Tried to translate.
    That doesn't shed
      a dimension.
Seven bells
   in turn
cracking
   the monk
    I played.
No longer has anything
I took
    in humble self-effacement

recognized
my bright
red tongue.
The tribal class
mistakenly powerful.
It's quaint
swooping manner
short
in a tall glass.
Dislocated,
but we will return
disconcerted to
a fine line.
Somewhere in between
don't cry.
You are left with the one
with blue cheese.
Get the gist.
Sometimes it's
a kind of pun
wearing ragged clothes.
Chant Colette.
Sing the dictionary,
improvise.
All will be
realized
in a conceptualized
brothel.
Feeling
a lot
of the familiar.
That performance,
dressed
in a wooden bathtub,
taped
in thinking things,
you sank
with a door
interpreting
weeping
wordless
willows.

## While Listening to the Lovers Next Door

The night left us with nowhere
to sit in the rain and just drown,
so we headed inside
where we turned on the radio
while listening to the lovers
                    next door.
When the sun came out
we were playing blind
man's bluff in the hallway
where there was no inkling
of the good and the bright.
We were sleepy by that point,
but, being that fair weather
is a rarity in this town
it was inevitable that we'd
do our punch dive down
                    into the street.
Everyone was muttering,
so their explanations
served no directional purpose.
Going to the museum
we immediately regretted not going
to the candy store on the last
corner where they sold the French
                    cigarettes.
By the time we came to the Vermeers
there was nothing to do but run quick
so that we would be able to catch
the last bit of fun far from the tourist park.
No one wanted to be there,
but we were the only ones
who were willing to make that point
                    known.
All the boys were looking at you weird,
lusting after your leopard skin coat
and the mystery wild haired beneath.
They figured that you'd take them
                    to the circus

and make it a simpler day,
dropping the unnecessary complexities
                        of skin.
The afternoon was bad for our health
and midnight wasn't much better,
but at least it wasn't raining.
There were stairwells that we wanted to climb
and so many keys on the chains that our parents
                        had left us
to fit into the keyholes on the cross streets.
At last we could run across the up and down
avenues so long on this island of broken red lights
                        stuck on green.

## Scar

You said that I would become
the knife to slit your throat,
but now all you have is a scar
and heartsick sobs that eclipse
        sun and moon.
I stand silent and empty handed.

We have no business wanting
the things we let pass.

# Flower

## I

I found a flower
lying on the back
        of my own
        past treasures,
        unchanging.

## II

        Streets pass,
            drop.
In the cities left
        behind there are
        too many empty vases.

## III

In the hair
of the flower vendor
        were lilac petals.
Her eyes caught mine.
My memories of spring scattered
        without tears.

## IV

At noon
I entered
            the perfumed restaurant
short the fortune
        necessary
for the waiter's
        eye,
        I did not
ask to be seated.

I stood at the table.

## V

Flower petals fell
       from her hair
as I stood
              watching.

## Table by a Window

No fork
but spoon
fill my glass
it is the hour
on the nose
on the clock
for cigarettes
black hearts
and flowers
to turn from
the light bulb
outside
by sunset
I will be
drunk
dead
spilled out
on the patterned
rug
while you rush
through squares
of shadows
on the street
below

# Sweet Lil

Sweet Lil drank from the mug of the beast and slept on the belly of the poet. She never left a tip that the barmaid found acceptable. The barmaid took what she could get, all the same. Sweet Lil caught a break because she was known for spreading a good word. Sweet Lil was a mute. She never let anyone know this. Naturally, the poet was left to starve while the mug was sucked dry. The barmaid never acquired enough cash for a decent dowry and died an old maid, much to Sweet Lil's delight.

## Siberian Breathless Song

Had she remained
   indifferent
      quite extraordinary
      spiders
         would have
            marched
         towards their extinction,
    but wanting
       to differentiate
autumn from spring
she sought
   compassion
in a darkened smile.
      Beneath wings
      dangling
    she listened
    to the excruciating
       Siberian
       breathless song
           with cryptic
               dissidents
    finally freed.
In the primordial dive
where the chow dogs
   pretended to understand
     the nuances
       that sputtered
         in the bird's eyes
she refilled her wine glass,
    and sang praises
of the piercing sights
seen by the woman
         wearing seven
         amethyst
         rings.
Toward the slippery light that filled
the last frozen and modified dream
   of the dying moment

                her enthused
left eye
                        moved
                                to observe
            the thaw
                                    and opened
            secrets left delinquent
in a field of supernatural eclipses
                that generated a history filled
                with cock and bull characters.
These characters
        ignited
    a sexual fascination
            in the midst of an orgasm
                    debate
    pursuing the melancholy smile
that belonged
        to the amethyst ringed woman
with tobacco blackened teeth.
She fell
        into the arms
            of undesirable eccentrics
            when summer
                    dropped
            into winter's well.

# Half Emptied Glass

There is nothing
more than a half emptied
glass of Chateauneuf du Pape
left on the wobbling table
to remind us of your exit,
and of how
little your breath
affected us.

Tomorrow I will
send a letter
to your children
in spite of the fact
that the calendar
points nowhere
near to Christmas.

I will tell
them how sorely
missed you
will be to some,
and not to
expect presents
from any of the jollier
sorts in the years
to come.

## Afternoon Transgression

I found
      myself
      lost
in the armor
of your eyes                        with a memory
                                    coughed up.
            You always said
            I was a gorgeous
                                          rodent
banished                       from the granaries of paradise
because of my lust
      for the chimera
of a cheese sandwich.

## Excuse

Flip the big excuse
On the pat reply.
           In ten minutes
       You'll hit the wall
When you realize
That the chef
Lost his thumb
           In an action
That most
Would not find
          Particularly
          Demanding
And that the head waiter
Spat up his noble title
In a bowl of Vichyssoise.

# Deli

Lovely
your tongue
          devours
     my eye
I lick
your
        salty
        black
        pupil
all of the dinners
that we have shared
with my father
the railroad engineer
will forever seem
culinarily suspect
when compared to Monday's
        lunch
in the ghetto deli
    that
       moved
           uptown
with its torn leather booths
and Formica tables
where we stood heroic
eating liverwurst and onion
        on rye
        waiting
        for sunset's
     conclusion
   in statistical hunger
observed by first year geometers
and commented on by algebraic scholars
        blindly following stars
        we make promises
         of forever
and content ourselves
with the cannibal reality
of finding lesser deities
ready to be home cooked

## My Fish Girl

My fish girl
I know why
      you float
amongst the wondrously
hued fish in the ocean
caught in the sky
      blue
your eyes are blue
beyond the sky
though the clouds
      pass by
the lighthouse
      far-off
awaits the lighting
of the night
for all the ships
      with sailors
who hope to never swim
amongst the fish and you
      who float
my fish girl
I know why
you don't swim

## The Floor Barren

The dancers had left
the floor barren,
and run off to the buffet table.
I would have run with them,
but my pockets were full,
something quite extraordinary,
especially for a Monday.

# Mystery of the Street

Once there was
a workman
a mother and child
a shovel and rubble
shadows
which longed
for the light
sweep
but those were
different times
times
of dead sciences
and alchemists
when everyone
looked up
to the sun
and the moon
and the stars
in the sky
now we simply
fall from heaven
face first

## Odysseus Disorientated

Weeping in the house on Saturday afternoons my mother would crown me with laurels and proclaim me to be Odysseus disorientated, and not merely a child escaped. I bathed in a white fountain and drowned hedgehogs in the foam of my joy that insinuated eternity. My mother would screech, finding me lost at sea. She surrounded me with mountains and sewed my mouth shut every spring with yellow thread. My greatest joys were to attend the funerals of old sailors and pig roasts. Since then all of the leaves have withered on my skull.

# Booth Reaction

Loving on the subway platform           we too poor
that is home                              mine
                                         yours
moving downtown                  and we            're
                                         maimed
you say                               we
                             ought
                     to catch a taxi upstate
                                         metered
see all of the mansions
and all the sybaritic gardens           of the Hudson Valley

There was sun this afternoon
All the girls ran out into it
But the boys preferred more accessible photographs
                                   It was an act of cruelty
                                   But not violence

on the Eighth Avenue Line          dropping from Inwood
your rid Λ sea                     not to be seen
                                   out     out     out
                             I don't want to transfer
                             I don't want to come up
above ground again
here we have air conditioning             and Spanish fans

At the turnstile                            we kissed
                            we broke
                            two
never looking back

## The Last Buck Passed

On the day that his mother
Passed the buck
Onto him he decided
That the best thing
To do was to go out
And put a bid
In on Meyer Lansky's
Brown shoelaces
Which he soon
Acquired with minimal
Controversy being
That the prime
Rival held only
Too bits and a black
Bread baguette
(Nowhere near enough).
When he brought
The shoelaces back
To his mother
Saying "this is what
You get when
You pass the last buck,"
She was anything
But elated
For she had known
Meyer Lansky well
From the stories
That her aunts
Would tell
While sitting
On her mother's
Brooklyn stoop
All of those years
Ago.
Having the inside
Scoop although long
Past still remembered
It was apparent

To her that these brown
Shoelaces never belonged
To that great financier,
But rather
To Dutch Schultz,
And that they had
Held tight his shoes
That long ago
Night in the blood
Bath diner.

She had always hated
Newark and these shoestrings
Held nothing but horrid
Memories of New Jersey
Nights that she
Had believed that she
Had long ago left
Behind.

She had nothing
But curses for him,
And the last buck
That she had
Passed.
Being the resilient
Type though
The mother that Russia
Had always longed
For, she took
The shoelaces tightly
In hands
And quickly did away with him.

## He was a Bald Man

He was a bald man,
        or at least I believe
that he was a bald man.
I don't remember a time
        when I saw him
without his beige fedora
        at a tilt.
I can no longer wear my hat
at a tilt because my hat
        is no longer my own.
I gave it to an anarchist one
        night, so that he would
not be blinded by the sun
when the bloody bombs of freedom
        were thrown.
I wish that I still had my
        hat.  The winter is coming,
my head is bare, my hair is
growing thin, and the tyrant is
        still on the throne.

# Cinema

Not so much free
        moviegoers
                search
affectionately
        for three weeks.
Quick shot
    of   gesticulating
                feminine
                hornets.
The new being,
        the filth
        who first
            duped paradise,
rolls obscenely,
comes out alone
        with iron cymbals
        in fingerless hands.
The dying clown.
The public
        shrugs its
            crabs loused
                shoulders.
You're leaving?
Going to Tibet?
Destroying my Himalayan body?
You're still here.
The pretext being
        cinema,
            but there is no
sounds of the countryside
        produced by a loudspeaker.
There is no bearable
        commercial lucidity.
Some cops burst
        in with excited
            high-pitched voices
giving shrill
        spurting screams.

Words
        gradually
  express
  pictorial values.
Breath is short.
Objects take
    their leap
      of brutal
self-transcendence.

## The Sailors' Sons

We are sons of sailors
who got lost inland
with no passion for the streets
that they found themselves
            wrecked on.
There's a sleepiness here.
The kind of sleepiness
that America loves
to feel in its wild hands tightened
around the gun of God
beautiful in the killing spree.
There's so much religion
now that there are no whales
            to pursue.
I, with my brothers bereft
at the sight of the lifeguards
sitting high and tan
in their ascendancy
will swim out beyond their seeing
to the seas of our betters.

# An Hour From the Burning Bush

Where I stood was an hour
from the burning bush
that's what the compass
and the guide book said
the sun was setting
and I was short of matches
so I was shit out of luck
I should have never fell in
with the Biblical scholars
who were always asking
me for the money for an egg
cream over on 2nd Avenue
the alchemists were better
behaved the kind of masters
that my mother would have
preferred to see me smoke
cigarettes with none of this
really mattered in the middle
of nowhere with Moses
far from sight and most likely
forgotten by everyone out
in the wilderness but myself

## Lecture II

Four reiterations.
    Nothing but numbers.
A new style
    not
        necessarily
reductive.
Creating
      heroes.
Collecting
    huge
Egyptian antiquities.
      The father
        on the
      mantelpiece.
No date
      for the deity's
        jealousy.
            Nail it shut.
Interaction.
      I can't pronounce
stone structures.
      Traditions
        parallel,
and transmute
      the ushers
        of nirvana
while picking up
   various household
        weird regards.
Holding
    its tongue,
and swallowing mentions,
periodically
      a printing press
will stop nurturing
      interpretations
        of footnotes, and offer
the royal road

for the breakage
of perplexing logic.
            Hysteria
                the first thing
in focus.
Slip of the
        ego state.
It won't
        repress
        the symbolic
coming out.
Between
        constructive
        primitivism
            and
        windows
            of residue
sits
            the immobile
                synthesis
                    of
numbers.
The prior
            strategy
was to erase
        a drawer.
No trace,
a wish to eradicate
            the act, but the
elaborate
        show
creeps up.  The
        jargon is
            wasted here.
Look into
    the jar
        on the bed.
Remember, evidence
        that is nothing
            is not
                darkness.

## Tea

The poker club has gone uptown for a Woodlawn picnic. They serve cucumber sandwiches on Saturdays and pour out cemetery steam in their tea cups on Sundays. They suffocate the hucksters who sell miracle tonics along bristling paths of the Bronx and toss lumps of cheer on the graves of the birthday babies.

## Ecstasy

Con
    SUME        The
                des
                      ire
    on the
      platter,

                              silver,

          THOUGH
tar
nished.
            As
            if
it were
            a
            for
gotten
        master
piece
in
            a
          broke
            N
museum.
Those who walk by know that there is nothing inside that they
                  either want, or need
        to
      see.
                No one
really
cares
        to
         look.

                Shall we
exit?
        Perhaps

        St

                OP
        by the Spanish
                joint
for
a
bite
of

                        ox
        TAIL.


Good, it seems so appropriate on a day like today, and if today is
        not
                appro
                        priate
        then we can always stop by again
                                tomorrow.

## Shark

Your shark appeared off of the shores of Western Africa while I was shaving. I heard screams and trimmed my nose hairs. All these people on the coast have to come up with a better way for making a living than fishing and gun running. All of these floundering revolutions turn to ashes. Even the cannibals starve here.

ARTEIDOLIA
PRESSPRESSPRESSPRESSPRESS

www.ingramcontent.com/pod-product-compliance
Lightning Source LLC
LaVergne TN
LVHW041307080426
835510LV00009B/885